THE AGE OF
SAILING SHIPS

USBORNE PUBLISHING

Acknowledgements
We wish to thank the following
individuals and organizations for
their assistance and for making
available material in their
collections.

Key to picture positions:
(T) top, (C) centre, (B) bottom,
(L) left, (R) right.

Associated Press: 11(T)
Buckler's Hard, Hampshire, photo
  Pitkin Pictorials: 19(T)
Michael Holford: 6(TR)
Illustrated London News: 44(T)
Mansell Collection: 11(CR) (BL)
Musée de la Marine, Paris, photo
  Jacqueline Hyde: 20(T)
National Maritime Museum. London:
  15(C), 28(B), 33(BL)
New York Historical Society: 16(T) (C)
Radio Times Hulton Picture Library
  10(L)
Rijksmuseum, Amsterdam: 11(BR)
St Louis Art Museum, Missouri: 15(T)
Science Museum, London, photo
  Brian Marshall: 21 (top five photos)
Tresco Abbey, Scilly Isles. photo
  G.P.B. Naish: 21 (bottom five photos)
Ulster Museum, Belfast: 12 (three
  photos)
Peter Wakeford: 36-37 (ship models),
  photos John Freeman

Illustrators

Roland Berry
Fred Burnley
Sydney Cornford (Gilchrist
  Studios)
Bill Easter
Gerry Embleton
Brian Lewis
Angus McBride
Peter Mousdale
Linda Nash
Keith Robson
Stobart·Sutterby
George Thompson
Jenny Thorne
Arthur Wakelin (Gilchrist
  Studios)

Editor
Jane Ades

Designer
Peter Wakeford

Picture Manager
Millicent Trowbridge

Typesetting
Purnell

Colour reproduction
Fotolitho Drommel, Zandvoort.
Holland

Made and printed in England by
W. S. Cowell Ltd, Butter Market,
Ipswich

First published in 1976 by
Usborne Publishing Ltd
20 Garrick Street
London WC2

Text and artwork © 1976 by
Usborne Publishing Limited

ISBN 0 86020 023 X

THE AGE OF
SAILING SHIPS

G.P.B. NAISH & HEATHER AMERY

CONTENTS

First Sailing Ships

This wooden Egyptian ship was about 75 ft long and 20 ft wide. It could sail with the wind but had to be rowed against it.

Greek warships had 23 oars in two banks on each side, which gave them the name of bireme. At the bow was an iron or bronze ram. This was used to hole enemy ships. A bireme was steered by an oar on each side at the stern.

Viking ships were built of oak and some were large enough to carry 300 men. A steering oar hung from the starboard, or right side, of the ship's stern.

The first cogs had one mast and a square sail. They were steered by a rudder, hinged to the stern of the ship. At the top of the rudder a lever, called a tiller, was moved by a helmsman to steer the ship. Cogs had extra decks at the bow and stern, called castles. These were used by soldiers when attacking other ships and also made cabins for the crew.

This galley carried pilgrims from Venice to the Holy Land in the 15th century. It had two masts with lateen sails and was rowed with long oars or sweeps when becalmed or making port.

Setting Sail

The story of sailing ships began about 6,000 years ago. No one knows who built the first ones but records of Ancient Egyptian sailing ships have been found. The Egyptians built reed boats for sailing on the River Nile. Later they used local wood and cedar wood imported from Lebanon for their sea-going ships. The planks of these wooden ships were joined with wooden nails and pegs. They had one mast with a very large rectangular sail and could sail only when the wind was blowing from behind them. To go in any other direction, the ships had to be rowed by men standing on the deck. The Egyptians made long voyages across the Mediterranean and the Red Sea at the time the pyramids were built. They brought back myrrh, incense trees, apes, ivory and gold.

Warships and Merchantmen

After the Egyptians, the Cretans and Phoenicians sent their trading ships all over the Mediterranean. They were followed by the Greeks. Until about 800 B.C. warships and merchantships looked very alike. Later, merchantships became larger so that they could carry more cargo, and warships were built for speed. The warships had two, three or five rows of oars on each side. They had a single mast with a square sail.

The Vikings

In Northern Europe, a different type of ship developed. These were built by the Vikings in the creeks of Scandinavia and were used to invade Christian Europe in the 9th and 10th centuries. The long, slim ships carried one mast, which could be raised and lowered, with a square sail. They were also rowed with long oars by men sitting on benches.

Four centuries later, larger, broader ships, called cogs, were built in Northern Europe. They had extra decks at each end, called castles, and a rudder hinged to the stern. At the same time, Mediterranean seafarers were using a different type of ship. This was the galley —a ship with three masts and many oars. Its triangular sails were called "lateen" sails, from the word "latin".

Building the Hull

From the earliest times, the hulls of Mediterranean ships were carvel built. This meant planks were laid smoothly edge to edge

Northern ships were clinker built. The lower edge of each plank overlapped the upper edge of the plank beneath it.

Ships to Sail Oceans

Here are two views of a typical mid-16th century ship. At that time, most merchant ships and warships looked alike. The high sterns were castles during battles. The four masts carried square and triangular sails. Such ships made great voyages of discovery, opening up the sea lanes of the world for trade and the spread of Western ideas and beliefs.

The pennant—a long ribbon-like flag which was flown from the main mast.

Main sail divided into two parts—the course and bonnet.

The bonnet is the extra strip of canvas which seamen could remove in bad weather in order to reduce the size of the sail.

▼Side view of a carrack.
1 Bowsprit
2 Bows
3 Forecastle
4 Foremast with foresail
5 Aftercastle

Main topsail

Fore topsail

Course

Bonnet

Flags of the ship's country or home port flew from the flagstaffs.

Main topsail yard

Armed men stood in the round platforms, called the tops, at the head of the main and fore masts.

Main yard

Men climbed up the ropes, called shrouds, which supported the masts.

Mizzen mast with lateen mizzen sail.

Block on running rigging.

Ropes used to set and furl the sails are called running rigging.

Heavy guns were mounted on the lower decks and their muzzles came out through the gun ports.

Stern of ship

Rudder

The hull is the body of the ship.

Anchors tied at the side while the ship was at sea.

1

4

3

2

Finding the Way

The ancient seafarers in the Mediterranean found their way by following the coastlines and islands, whose outlines were drawn in books of pilotage directions, as landmarks. When out of sight of land, they relied on their knowledge of the direction of the winds and waves at different times of the year and on the sun, moon and the stars.

Sailors who ventured across the Atlantic in the 16th century had no accurate charts. They used a simple compass to find the north and estimated the distance travelled by keeping a record of how fast the ship sailed. They also had to take into account the winds and tides that pushed their ships off a straight course. This method of navigation, known as "dead reckoning", was not very accurate.

Sailors could find out their latitude—how far they were north or south of the equator—with instruments such as the cross-staff, backstaff or astrolabe. With these they measured the height of the midday sun or a star, usually the Pole Star, above the horizon. With the help of tables, first published in Lisbon in 1509, they could work out their ship's latitude. This was the beginning of scientific navigation.

The Lead

The traverse board was hung up in front of the helmsman. He marked with pegs the course he had steered and the distance he estimated the ship had travelled every half-hour.

The lead, tied to the end of a rope, was thrown by the leadsman.

The leadsman wore an apron tied to the ship's rigging. This kept him dry and left both hands free. When the lead hit the seabed he called out the depth of the water in fathoms.

The line is marked off in fathoms with bits of cloth, rope and leather which look and feel different to the leadsman.

The lead weighs between 7 and 14 lbs and is attached to 25 fathoms of thin rope.

Tallow in the hollowed-out bottom of the lead picks up samples from the seabed.

The lead is the oldest known navigational instrument. A cylinder of lead is tied to the end of a long, thin rope, called the lead line, which is marked at intervals of so many fathoms. A fathom is equal to 6 ft and, until recently, was used to measure the depth of water by English-speaking countries. The leadsman coiled up the line and threw the lead well ahead, to allow for the ship moving forward. As the line ran through his fingers, he noted the marks. When the lead hit the seabed, he called out the number of fathoms of line which had run out. Sticky tallow, or grease, in the hollowed-out bottom of the lead picked up sand, small stones or mud and indicated what type of seabed the ship was sailing over.

The Log

Steering by the Stars

The cross-staff was a stick, with a sliding cross piece, which came into use in the 15th century. A sailor slid the cross piece along the staff, which was marked in sections, until he could see the horizon level with the lower end of the cross piece and the sun or star against the upper end of the cross piece. The observer then read off the mark which measured the angle between the horizon and the star. From this, he could work out the latitude of his ship—that is, its position north or south of the Equator.

Cross-staff

Backstaff

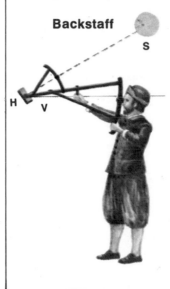

The observer stood with his back to the sun (S) to use the backstaff. He looked at the horizon (H) through a slit in the horizon vane on the end of the staff (V). The sun cast the shadow of the vane on the smaller arc on to the horizon vane which was now sighted on the horizon.

By adding the angles measured on the two arcs, the observer found out the sun's height over the horizon. The backstaff avoided the glare of the sun's rays but the cross-staff was still needed on cloudy days.

Sailors used the log to measure a ship's speed. The log was a flat piece of wood, weighted with lead on one side so that it floated upright in the water. The log was dropped over the stern of a ship and stayed almost stationary in the water while the ship moved forward. A line attached to the log was marked at regular intervals with knots. By counting the number of knots paid out in a fixed time, measured by a sandglass, a sailor could work out the ship's speed. He gave this in "knots", which came to mean "sea miles per hour".

A simpler method was to drop a piece of wood over the bows of a ship and time how long the whole of the ship took to pass it. This was called the Dutchman's log.

The Compass

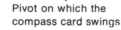

Rings, called gimbals, which tilt with the movement of the ship to keep the compass always upright.

Pivot on which the compass card swings.

The compass card, or rose, is marked with 32 points or wind directions.

It is likely that the compass was invented by the Chinese. They certainly knew that a magnetized needle points north. In Europe in the 12th century, a piece of straw with a magnetized needle in it was floated in a bowl of water to find the north. This apparatus was set up when necessary to check a ship's course. Later the needle was mounted on a pivot so it could swing easily. Then sailors glued the magnetized needle to a round card, marked

with 32 points. This became the compass card, or rose. The compass was put in a box with a glass top to protect it. The inside of the box of a ship's compass was marked with a line, or lubber's mark, which must be exactly in line with the ship's keel. When the helmsman was given a direction to sail in, he turned the ship so the point on the compass card was over the lubber's mark. Keeping them together, he steered a straight course.

Discovering the World

By 1400, Europeans knew of the existence of about half the world. Their world, which was thought to be flat, stretched east from Newfoundland, across the Atlantic, Europe and north Africa to Japan. By the 1700s, men had sailed across the oceans and had explored the coastlines of all the continents.

In 1494 the Pope drew up a treaty which divided the world. All lands discovered west of the 1494 line went to Spain; the rest, including Newfoundland and Brazil, to Portugal.

New Sea Routes

This map shows the routes taken across the world by early European explorers. It also shows some of the foods, birds and animals never seen by Europeans before, and the goods they found for trade. These voyages opened the way for the setting up of new overseas colonies. In trade and empires, the Portuguese explorers led the other countries.

Fishing grounds off Newfoundland.

From North America came beaver fur, timber, potatoes, maize, tobacco turkeys and gold.

Christopher Columbus saw Indians wearing gold and pearls on his early voyages.

1578 Drake

1567 De Mendana

ATLANTIC OCEAN

1492 Columbus

Sugar cane

PACIFIC OCEAN

Francis Drake sailed round the world in the *Golden Hind*.

Silver

Cacao bean

Silver

Llama carrying silver for export.

Spanish explorers set out from Peru to explore the Pacific and the legendary southern continent.

Equator

1567 De Mendana

Pineapple

1595 De Mendana

Cacao bean

1605 Quiros and de Torres

Brazil wood

1642 Tasman

1519-22 Magellan and del Cano

1578 Drake

1494 line

The *Victoria* was the first ship to sail round the world. Its captain, **Ferdinand Magellan**, died in the Philippines and Sebastian del Cano took charge. Only 18 of the expedition's 234 men returned home to Spain. The voyage lasted three years.

Many people believed there was a vast land mass to the south of the American continent. **Spanish explorers** and **Abel Tasman**

8

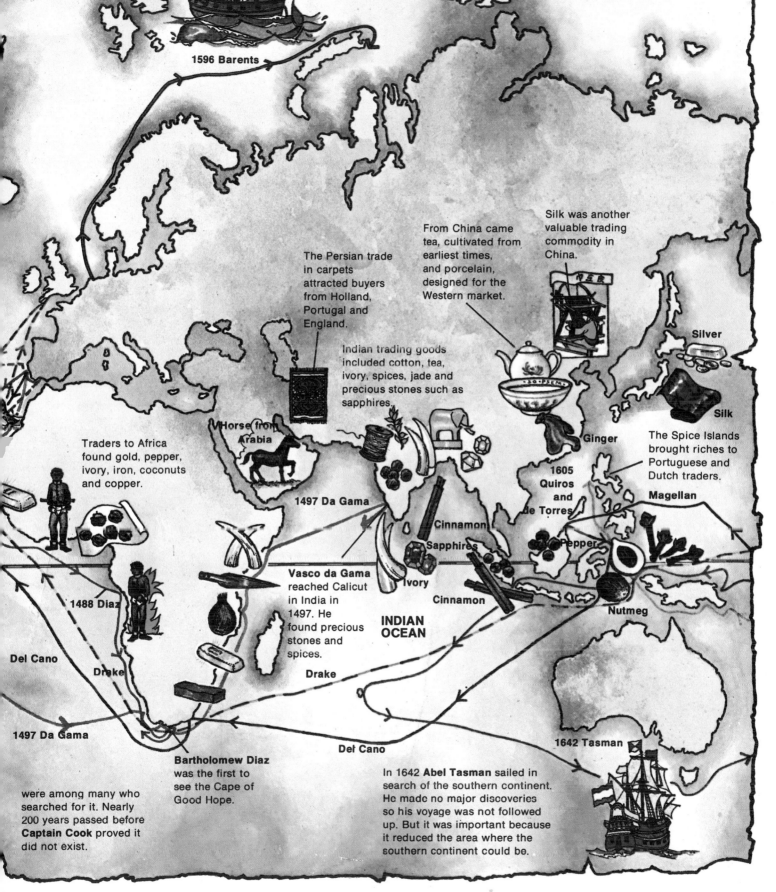

Willem Barents spent the winter at Novaya Zemlya in the Arctic circle. His crew returned to Holland with reports of whaling grounds.

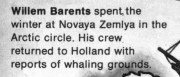

1596 Barents

The Persian trade in carpets attracted buyers from Holland, Portugal and England.

From China came tea, cultivated from earliest times, and porcelain, designed for the Western market.

Silk was another valuable trading commodity in China.

Indian trading goods included cotton, tea, ivory, spices, jade and precious stones such as sapphires.

Silver

Silk

Ginger

The Spice Islands brought riches to Portuguese and Dutch traders.

Traders to Africa found gold, pepper, ivory, iron, coconuts and copper.

Horse from Arabia

1497 Da Gama

1605 Quiros and de Torres

Magellan

Cinnamon

Sapphires

Pepper

Vasco da Gama reached Calicut in India in 1497. He found precious stones and spices.

Ivory

Cinnamon

INDIAN OCEAN

Nutmeg

1488 Diaz

Del Cano

Drake

Drake

1497 Da Gama

Del Cano

1642 Tasman

Bartholomew Diaz was the first to see the Cape of Good Hope.

were among many who searched for it. Nearly 200 years passed before **Captain Cook** proved it did not exist.

In 1642 **Abel Tasman** sailed in search of the southern continent. He made no major discoveries so his voyage was not followed up. But it was important because it reduced the area where the southern continent could be.

9

Early Explorers

Portuguese sailors were the first to make long journeys of exploration. Henry, the son of the King of Portugal, captured Ceuta in Morocco, on the north African coast, from the Moors in 1415. This led to a series of voyages down the west coast of Africa.

Henry left his father's court and founded a centre of navigation and research at Sagres in southern Portugal. He employed men to design ships, draw maps and charts, and study astronomy. Unfortunately, they kept their knowledge to themselves, so other sailors could not benefit from it.

During Henry's lifetime, Portuguese sailors discovered and charted the Atlantic Islands of Madeira, the Azores and Cape Verde. They also reached Sierra Leone, 1,500 miles down the west African coast.

The Portuguese voyages continued and, in 1488, Bartholomew Diaz sailed round the Cape of Good Hope on the tip of Africa and some way up the east coast. The sea route to India was now open. Nine years later, Vasco de Gama reached Calcutta, the major port for the spice trade.

Westwards to India

Christopher Columbus, who was born in Italy, was sure he could reach India by sailing westwards across the Atlantic. Financed by the king and queen of Spain, he claimed all the lands he discovered on his four voyages between 1492 and 1504 for that country.

On his first voyage he set out with three ships and sighted the Bahamas. He was sure they were Indian islands and for this reason the islands off the west coast of America are called the West Indies. On later voyages he discovered the mainland of South America and explored the Gulf of Mexico.

Ferdinand Magellan, a Portuguese navigator, also offered his services to Spain. In 1519 he set out with five ships to find a way westwards. He discovered a strait between Patagonia and Tierra del Fuego (which was later named after him) and sailed into the Pacific. Crossing the vast ocean, he reached the Philippines. There he died but one of his ships returned to Spain—the first to sail round the world—after a voyage lasting three years.

Magellan's journey proved that there was a route across the Pacific to the East. Other explorers set out from the Spanish colony in Peru. Alvaro de Mendana discovered the Solomon Islands, which stretched for 600 miles. On a later voyage, he could not find them again but discovered a group of islands, called Les Marquesas de Mendoza and settled on the volcanic island of Santa Cruz. Mendana died but his companion, Pedro Fernandez de Quiros, took the expedition on to Manila in the Philippines.

In 1605, Quiros set out again from Peru with Luis Vaez de Torres in search of an unexplored land which geographers at that time believed lay to the south of the American continent. This was the first of many voyages in search of the legendary continent. They continued until Captain Cook proved it did not exist, nearly 200 years later.

▲ **Prince Henry was the patron** of Portuguese explorers and financed several expeditions down the West African coast.

▶ **Caravels were the most successful discovery ships** of the 15th century. Developed in Portugal from fishing boats, they were light, fast and could be sailed in all winds. Caravels were sailed by Henry the Navigator's explorers on their great ocean voyages. The ships could cut through Atlantic waves and were shallow enough to sail close to shores.

The Golden Hind

This is a replica of the *Pelican*, renamed the *Golden Hind*. It was the ship in which Sir Francis Drake reached California, on the west coast of North America, in 1497. The original ship was about 102 ft long and was probably built of seasoned oak.

The replica was the result of long, careful research. It took three years to build at a ship-yard in Devon, England. As oak is now difficult to obtain, the hull was made of an African hardwood, called iroko. But in all other ways, the ship was as correct as possible in every detail – the sails and rigging, furniture and weapons.

The new *Golden Hind* was launched on 5 April, 1973. It was sailed from England across the Atlantic to its final mooring in San Francisco in 1974. There it will be a permanent reminder of Drake's landing nearby.

Northeast to China

Willem Barents was perhaps the greatest of the Dutch Arctic explorers. He made three journeys, hoping to find a northeast trade route to China. The easier routes round Africa and South America were in the hands of the Portuguese and Spanish. In 1596, Barents set out from Amsterdam, in Holland, with two ships. They reached Spitzbergen, where one ship stayed, while Barents went on in the other. His ship was trapped in the ice off the coast of northern Russia and Barents and his crew were forced to spend ten months in the Arctic. They built a wooden hut on the island of Novaya Zemlya, living on food they rescued from the ship. When the ice melted, the explorers escaped in two open boats but Barents died on the way. The weary survivors reached home, bringing news of the many huge whales they had seen in the cold waters of the Arctic.

▲ **Barents's ship was trapped** by ice in the Arctic. His men used sleds to carry driftwood from the shore across the ice to an inland site where they built a hut for the winter.

◀ **The crew made the hut** as comfortable as possible. They cooked food over wood fires and used grease from polar bears as fuel for lamps. For many months they looked after their dying leader.

▶ **The ship's clock** was put up in the hut. The crew took everything they could carry from the ship. Musical instruments, clothes and cooking pots were found in the hut in 1871 by later explorers.

Armada Galleons

Laden with gold and silver from Mexico and Peru, Spanish ships sailed home across the Atlantic from 1564 onwards. Philip 11, the king of Spain, sent powerful warships to accompany these fleets and protect them from the pirates who set out to capture the treasure. The warships were galleons—well-armed fighting ships which had been developed by the Portuguese and were adopted by both Spain and England.

The Spanish Fleet

Philip sent a fleet of 130 ships, including many galleons, against England in 1588. This armada was to attack Queen Elizabeth for her support of the rebels in the Spanish Netherlands, for encouraging her sailors to plunder Spanish ships, and to convert Protestant England back to the Roman Catholic faith.

The fleet reached Calais, in northern France, and anchored to await an army to invade England. During the night, the English sent fireships—small ships well ablaze—drifting with the tide amongst the Spanish Armada. The fleet cut their anchor cables and scattered. Next day the Spanish and English ships met in battle off the coast of Flanders but a change in the wind saved the armada. It set off for home, leaving a trail of ships wrecked off the rocky coasts of northern Scotland and Ireland.

Armada Treasure

These gold jewels, from a gentleman's outfit, are part of the treasure recovered from the wreck of the *Girona* after nearly 400 years. The ship was one of the Spanish fleet and was wrecked off the coast of Ireland during a storm. Of a crew of 1,300, only five men survived.

In 1968 and 1969 a team of French and Belgian divers spent 6,000 hours underwater. Nothing of the ship itself remained but they raised instruments, guns, coins and silver tableware.

1 This is the back of a gold jewel in the shape of a salamander. The lizard-like creature was thought to be able to live in fire, so the charm was probably meant to bring good luck to its owner.

2 A Knight of Malta's gold cross which belonged to Fabricio Spinola. He was the captain of the *Girona* and came from Italy.

3 This gold jewel for a hat is set with pearls.

The Fighting Ship

This is a galleon. It was the strongest and most powerful of the ships used by both Spain and England during the unsuccessful Armada campaign.

Galleons were longer and narrower than earlier ships. They usually had four masts and were about 140 ft long. They carried between 30 and 80 guns, some of them very small ones. A ship's company was made up of 300 fighting seamen and 125 soldiers.

1 Trumpets were kept in a cabin at the stern. They were blown to salute passing ships or as a sign of defiance.

2 The captain's cabin was at the stern, the best room on board. It was light and airy with stern windows.

3 The gunroom was at the stern. Galleons carried heavy artillery. Gun ports were introduced about 1500. This meant heavy guns could be carried low in the ship. During the Battle of the Armada, ships fired guns broadside (all at once).

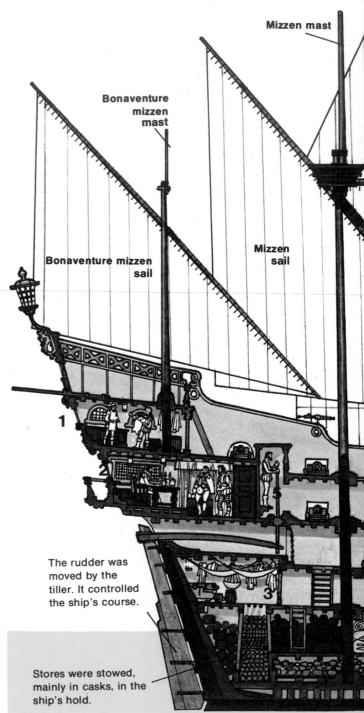

Mizzen mast

Bonaventure mizzen mast

Bonaventure mizzen sail

Mizzen sail

The rudder was moved by the tiller. It controlled the ship's course.

Stores were stowed, mainly in casks, in the ship's hold.

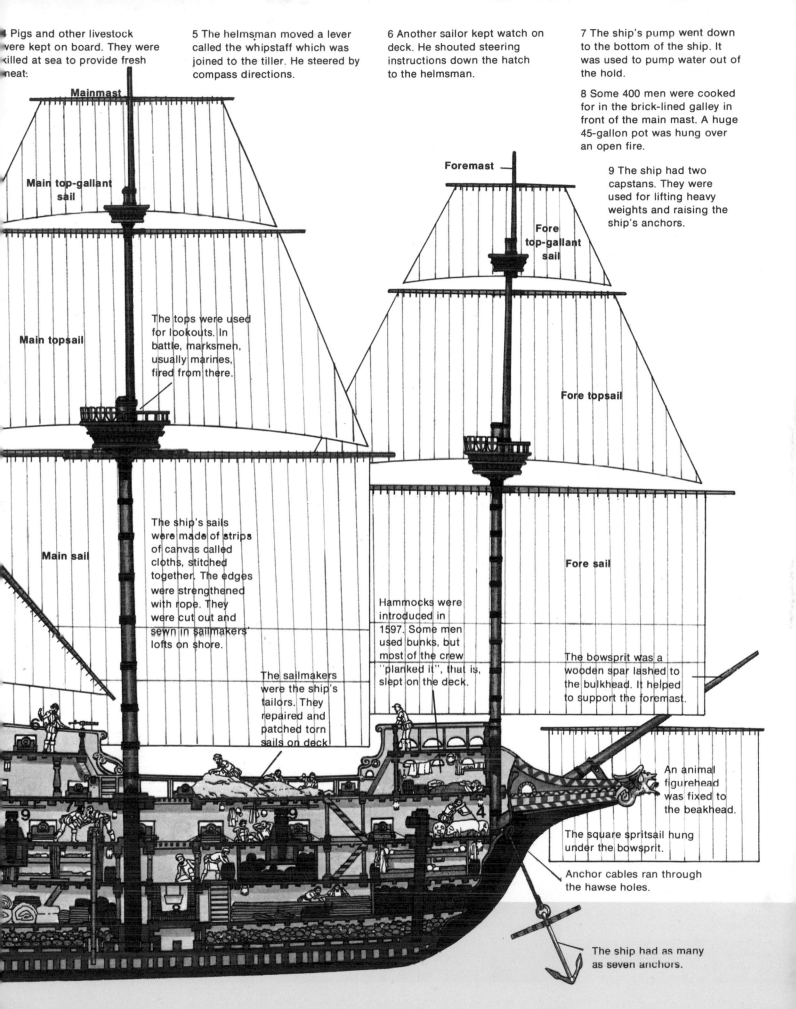

4 Pigs and other livestock were kept on board. They were killed at sea to provide fresh meat.

5 The helmsman moved a lever called the whipstaff which was joined to the tiller. He steered by compass directions.

6 Another sailor kept watch on deck. He shouted steering instructions down the hatch to the helmsman.

7 The ship's pump went down to the bottom of the ship. It was used to pump water out of the hold.

8 Some 400 men were cooked for in the brick-lined galley in front of the main mast. A huge 45-gallon pot was hung over an open fire.

9 The ship had two capstans. They were used for lifting heavy weights and raising the ship's anchors.

Mainmast

Main top-gallant sail

Main topsail

Main sail

The tops were used for lookouts. In battle, marksmen, usually marines, fired from there.

The ship's sails were made of strips of canvas called cloths, stitched together. The edges were strengthened with rope. They were cut out and sewn in sailmakers' lofts on shore.

The sailmakers were the ship's tailors. They repaired and patched torn sails on deck.

Foremast

Fore top-gallant sail

Fore topsail

Fore sail

Hammocks were introduced in 1597. Some men used bunks, but most of the crew "planked it", that is, slept on the deck.

The bowsprit was a wooden spar lashed to the bulkhead. It helped to support the foremast.

An animal figurehead was fixed to the beakhead.

The square spritsail hung under the bowsprit.

Anchor cables ran through the hawse holes.

The ship had as many as seven anchors.

13

Trade with the East

Explorers from Spain and Portugal were the first to bring back to Europe valuable cargoes of spices from the East Indies. The Dutch and English soon followed them and set up trading companies in the Far East in the 17th century. Large fleets of merchant ships were built to carry the cargoes.

The Dutch East India Company, formed in 1602, was backed by the state. It soon became the most important power in the Indian Ocean with a capital at Batavia on the island of Java. The company acted almost like an independent state—it built fortresses, fought wars and made treaties.

Battle for Trade

English merchants copied the Dutch and set up the East India Company with a charter from Queen Elizabeth I. The company was at first smaller than the Dutch one, with expeditions only every two or three years.

England's attempts to share the spice trade of the East Indies led to a massacre of English merchants by the Dutch in the Molucca Islands in 1623. After this, the English withdrew to the Indian mainland. The bases of the two companies were then firmly and successfully established.

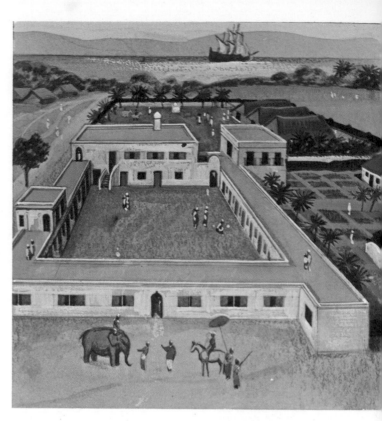

▲ **The Dutch and English** set up trading posts, or "factories" in the Far East near the main ports and harbours.

Using local materials, they built houses, often surrounded by high walls to protect the people and their goods.

A Port in the Far East

This is a busy harbour in the Dutch East Indies in the 17th century. Cages of live poultry, baskets of fresh fruit, bales of cloth and boxes of every kind of spice have been brought to the quay. Porters, carrying the goods on their heads, will load them into the small boats. These will be rowed out to the waiting ships and taken on board for shipment to the ports of Europe.

When the Dutch first reached the area in 1596, they set up a trading post on the island of Java. The Dutch East India Company, formed in 1602, became so powerful it was almost a state in itself. It built fortresses for defence and made its own treaties. Its administrators, like those of the English East India Company, were sometimes corrupt and dishonest. They were paid low wages while abroad and were expected to make the extra money necessary to live in comfort in the tropics. For a man with ability, there was a good career and perhaps a fortune to be made in the Far East.

Fishing Wars

The United Provinces of the Netherlands and England both felt they had the right to sail on all seas, trade with all nations and fish on all coasts. During the 17th century, disputes over these rights ended in war between the two countries. The Dutch controlled the North Sea fisheries. They had a huge fleet of 1,000 fishing boats.

The fishing boats, called busses, had three masts with a square sail on each one. They fished with nets for herring, haddock, cod and ling. Some of the fish were pickled in barrels of brine for export, others were brought fresh or smoked to the Dutch ports.

Dutch ships also carried huge quantities of cargo between the countries of Europe and the colonies. In 1651 a law was passed in England that all goods imported into the country must be carried in English ships or in ships of the country of origin. This was a direct threat to the Dutch carrying trade.

Rivalries between the Dutch and English increased. There were disputes over the herring fisheries, the whale fisheries in the Arctic, and the valuable East Indies spice trade. War broke out in 1652. The Dutch had more men and ships but their ships were not as large as the English ships. Both sides won victories but in the end England gained better terms.

▲ **Sea captains in Surinam,** a Dutch colony in South America.

By the 18th century, the Dutch had built up a huge empire.

▶ **Michael de Ruyter** was probably the greatest of the Dutch admirals. He began his naval career as a cabin boy when he was only 11 years old.

He played a leading part in the three wars between the Dutch and the English. In 1667 he organized a daring attack on England. Dutch ships sailed up the river Medway and captured the English warship, the *Royal Charles*. In 1676 he was killed fighting the French in the Mediterranean.

Travelling by Sea

Passengers in ancient times travelled on merchant ships which were sailing where they wanted to go. There were no ships especially for passengers. A sea traveller made arrangements with a ship's captain and agreed on the price to be paid to him. Even in the 16th and 17th centuries, the adventurous wishing to visit the newly-discovered lands travelled in crowded, uncomfortable conditions, eating bad food and often suffering from the common shipboard diseases. At that time, few people went on long ocean voyages, although some used the coastal trading ships.

In the late 18th and early 19th centuries, the new colonies in India and the Far East and in America led to an increase in sea travel. The rich paid for cabins which were built for them in the ships and which they furnished themselves. Those who could not afford such luxuries lived in cramped quarters on dormitory decks with few comforts on the long voyages. By the middle of the 19th century, the number of passengers increased, swelled by emigrants going to America and Australia. The amount of mail carried by ships also increased and more frequent sailings were needed. The ship owners had to open offices to cope with the number of people booking passages and to issue tickets.

The new fast clipper ships had permanent cabins and much more space for passengers. Some even had one or more bathrooms with cold seawater baths. As with all sailing ships on long voyages, no timetables could be fixed. The ships' masters used the trade winds and monsoons at different seasons. Adverse winds and rough seas could add weeks or even months to an ocean voyage. When reliable steamships were introduced on the main passenger routes, they provided regular services on fixed schedules and the sailing ships soon lost the passenger trade.

▲ **Wealthy passengers** on merchant ships lived in great style and comfort. They had private cabins and took their servants with them. On board a ship in 1816, a steward cleans a cabin, watched by a nurse, while the child plays with a doll.

▼ **This is a self-portrait**, drawn by the Baroness Hyde de Neuville in 1816. She lies in her bunk on board the *L'Eurydice*, listening to her daughter reading. The bunk seems to have wooden doors that can be closed and locked.

Life on board was not always pleasant for the passengers. In a storm, while the seamen worked on deck to reduce the sails and control the ship, the passengers had to stay below. During meals, the food slid off the tables and people were thrown about when the ship lurched over big waves. Sometimes the deck leaked and water flooded into the cabins. There was always the danger that the ship might be wrecked on a rocky coast and the passengers and crew drowned.

Passengers on Ships

A merchant ship is moored against a quay at a busy port. The wealthy passengers arrive in coaches just before the ship is due to sail. Their chests of clothes and goods are carried to their cabins. The cargo has already been lifted onto the deck and lowered through hatches into the holds. It is stowed in the lowest part of the ship. The last few casks of fresh drinking water and preserved food are loaded on board.

Carpenters at work on the cabin of a wealthy passenger. The slatted panels let air in but cannot be seen through.

▼ Passengers brought their own furniture aboard to furnish their cabins. It was often sold when they reached their destination.

▼ Some passengers preferred to sleep in swinging cots rather than fixed bunks. The cots were like wooden trays with mattresses.

▼ Cows, pigs and sheep were carried on the decks of ships. They provided fresh milk and meat during long voyages.

Fights sometimes broke out in small crowded ships. The passengers lived uncomfortably close together for as long as eight or nine months and became bored and irritable. The captain had to settle all quarrels and his word was law on his ship.

▼ Some crew were seasick at the start of voyages. After a few days, they became used to the ship's motion. Sick crew were punished when they did not work.

▼ Attempts were made to grow vegetables and fruit on the decks of some ships to provide fresh food. They were tended and watered by one of the crew.

In calm fine weather, the passengers enjoyed concerts on the poop deck. They also danced and played cards to pass the time.

"Crossing the line" was a ceremony held when a ship crossed the Equator. "King Neptune" held court and passengers were ducked.

Building Wooden Ships

The ancient wooden ships were built by skilled men who had few plans or drawings to follow. They relied on their knowledge of traditional ships to build seaworthy craft, gradually developing new hull shapes and adopting ideas for masts and sails. Later, detailed plans were drawn before a ship was begun. Models, made from these plans, were shown to the people who wanted a ship. The ship models were still made after naval architects had learned to draw accurate plans of ships. The three plans, showing the ship from one side, from above, and sections at various stages, were used to make full-scale drawings from which the wood was cut to size and shape.

The best wood for building large ships was oak. It was strong and did not rot quickly. A large warship needed 2,000 oak trees over 100 years old. New wood warped and split when put into a ship, so the felled trees were sawn up and left out in the rain and sun to season.

As well as the carpenters, or shipwrights, many skilled craftsmen were needed for building and fitting out a ship. The mast and spar makers cut the huge masts out of separate pieces of timber, slotting and binding them together. The smiths forged anchors, up to 20 ft long. The sailmakers laboriously cut out and stitched the canvas sails. The ropemakers spun yarn, smearing the ropes with tar, and the blockmakers made blocks for a ship's rigging.

▼**Naval architects** drew the plans of a ship. Full-scale drawings were made from them.

The timber was cut out, using these drawings as a guide. The pieces were later fitted together.

▼**The shipwrights** went to the forests to select the particular shapes of timber they needed.

The shapes were very carefully cut out to avoid wasting the old, well-seasoned oak or elm.

▼**The sawyers** used a large, double-ended saw to cut up the long lengths of wood.

▼**A shipwright's tools** were very simple. He used an axe for trimming wood and an adze for

shaping, trimming and finishing. A saw was used to cut timber and an auger for boring holes.

▼**The keel** of a new ship was laid on slips. The side timbers were bolted onto the keel.

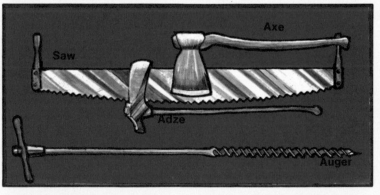
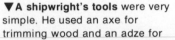

▼ **When the frame** of a ship was completed, it was covered with planks, laid edge to edge. They were fixed with wooden pins.

▼ **The planks of a ship** were made watertight by opening the seams with a special chisel and hammering in cotton rope.

▼ **Thin, overlapping sheets of copper** were nailed to ships' hulls sailing to the West Indies and in other warm seas after

1770. This was to prevent teredo worms, which live in warm sea water, from boring holes in the hulls of wooden ships.

A model of the shipyard at Buckler's Hard, on the south coast of England, as it would have been in 1803. One naval ship is ready for launching. The masts and rigging would have been added when it was afloat. The frame of a second ship on the slipway is almost finished and the sides and decks ready for the planks. Timber cut in the nearby oak forests awaits cutting.

Sheers were spars lashed together and used like a crane to lift masts onto a new ship.

Ropes of hemp were made by a spinner. He walked backwards, twisting the threads as he went.

The sailmaker cut out long strips of canvas to the required shape and stitched them together. He sewed rope round the sides and corners of a sail and moulded it with mallets.

Wooden pulley blocks were used on ropes which hoisted the sails and lifted cargo. They reduced the strain of the loads.

A ship's anchors were made by blacksmiths. They cast the iron shapes and welded them together at a dockyard forge.

A ship's bottom had to be scraped clean regularly. The ship was sailed on to a beach at high tide. When the water went down, burning reeds were used to loosen the barnacles and weeds which grew on the bottom and slowed the ship down.

Carving and Gilding

Gilded carvings, elaborate figureheads and splendid coats-of-arms on ships were important to European sailors of the late 16th and 17th centuries. They sometimes complained about the extra weight of an ornamental hull but still expected it. Such displays of the shipwrights' skill had no useful purpose but were there merely for show. From earliest times, ships often had some decoration, perhaps to show contempt for the enemy and to encourage the crew.

The ships owned by a king or a state were magnificently and expensively decorated. They reflected the art and architecture of the country where they were made.

The *Wasa* was built in Stockholm by Dutch shipwrights for the Swedish king and was splendidly decorated by Swedish carvers. The ship sank in the harbour on her first voyage in 1628. In 1961 the hull was lifted out of the mud and over 700 pieces of sculpture and ornament were recovered.

In the 18th century, the fashion changed and the decoration was much simpler. Today a few sailing ships have painted figureheads. This, with some decoration round the stern, is all that remains of an art which reached its height in the 17th century.

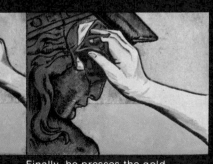

▲ **The stern of the 17th century ship**, the *Louis Quinze*. This model was probably used to teach young French royal children about the sea. The full sized ship was never built.

▶ **Seawater has removed** most of the colour and gilding from these wooden carvings, recently recovered from the wreck of the 17th century ship, the *Wasa*.

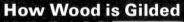

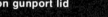

Huge lion figurehead

Lion's face on gunport lid

Roman warrior

Old man on a bracket

How Wood is Gilded

The gilder cleans the carvings and brushes on a coat of special glue.

He picks up a paper-thin sheet of beaten gold, called gold leaf, with a brush.

He dabs on the gold leaf and presses it into the carved shapes and cracks.

Finally, he presses the gold leaf down, smoothing it with a soft cloth wad.

These are details of a 3 ft dockyard model of the 17th century warship, H.M.S. Prince. At that time, ornate models were made and presented for approval before the order was placed and work began in the shipyard.

Enough of these models exist to provide a good record of what ships were like at that time. This model shows how much carved and gilded work decorated a ship of the period.

H.M.S. Prince was launched at Chatham, in England, in 1670. A well-armed man-of-war, it carried a crew of 780 when in home waters.

Bows with gilded horseman

Stern with royal arms and lanterns

Quarter gallery and wreathed gunports

Gilded figures guarding the entry port

Carved men and cherub on stern and quarter gallery

Wide stern windows of the captain's room

H.M.S. Prince was badly damaged during a successful battle with the Dutch when it was the flagship of the Lord High Admiral of England. The ship was broken up in 1692 but some timber was used to build another ship.

Figureheads

Many ships have been wrecked near the rocky Isles of Scilly, off southwest England. Many 19th century figureheads have been salvaged and are on show in the gardens of Tresco Abbey.

A Roman	A chieftain	Jane Owen	Roseville	Unknown lady

Science at Sea

The Pacific Ocean covers about one third of the earth's surface. Until 1700, most of it was unexplored and maps of it were blank. Many people in Europe believed there was a huge continent in the south Pacific but because of the prevailing westerly winds and inaccurate navigation its existence had never been proved. During the 18th century, explorers set out to chart the vast ocean. New instruments and tables enabled them to navigate accurately and return to a particular island or place on a coast once it had been charted.

Captain James Cook was perhaps the greatest explorer of his time. A merchant seaman, he became an officer in the British navy and was given command of three expeditions. He surveyed New Zealand and the east Australian coast: he discovered Hawaii and charted 3,000 miles of the west coast of North America. He also ended the myth of the continent in the south Pacific but found the cold, uninhabited wastes of Antarctica. His voyages opened the way for merchant shipping and the colonization of Australia.

Seamen on long voyages fell ill and sometimes died from a horrible disease called scurvy. It was not known until this century that it is caused by a lack of vitamin C which is found in fresh fruit and vegetables. James Cook carried bottles of fruit juice on his expeditions and better food for his crews. He also insisted on great cleanliness in his ships. He did not know the reason but was delighted that his men remained healthy on his voyages.

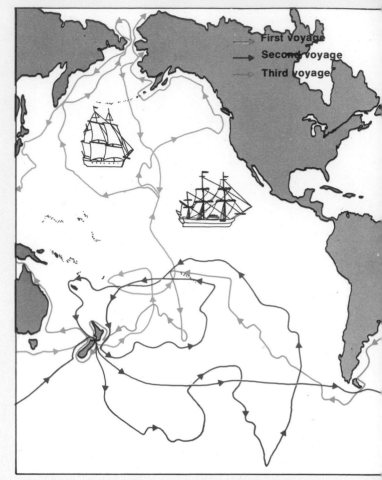

First Voyage
Second voyage
Third voyage

Captain James Cook surveyed and charted thousands of miles of the unexplored Pacific Ocean during his three voyages.

The Sailor's Food

Food on long sea voyages was dull and unhealthy. Fresh meat and vegetables quickly rotted. The cheese was soon alive with maggots and the butter went rancid. Rats gnawed the food casks and weevils infested the flour and biscuits. A sailor's diet consisted of beef and pork preserved in barrels of brine, dried fish, dried peas and a type of hard bread, called ship's biscuit. The fresh water turned green with scum.

New ways of preserving food were introduced in the 18th century and greatly improved the sailor's diet. Cabbage was pickled and packed in salt. Fruit juice was bottled and fresh fruit bought when a ship was in port. There was also condensed malt, and cakes of dried, compressed soup. The next improvement came in 1806 when the French navy introduced meat in glass containers—the forerunner of tinned food.

Cheese

Beer

Wine

Weevil

Dried fish

Butter

Rat

Ship's biscuits

Maggot

Sides of meat

Condensed malt

Pickled cabbage

Fresh fruit

Cakes of soup

Exploring and Charting Unknown Lands

Explorers in the Pacific in the 18th century gathered information on a wide range of subjects. They observed the stars and charted much of the ocean and some of the coastlines. They collected plants and animals and studied the people and customs.

1 A quadrant or a sextant was used to measure the angle of the sun, moon or stars. With the help of tables, a seaman could work out his ship's longitude—its position east or west of a fixed meridian.

2 A tent protected Cook's regulator clock from the sun. It was used with the sextant to calculate longitude.

3 Cook's marine chronometer was taken during his second and third voyages. It was used with the regulator clock and a quadrant or sextant to calculate the ship's longitudinal position.

4 An azimuth compass was used on deck to sight landmarks through the two upright vanes. Charts of coastlines were compiled with the help of these measurements.

5 Boats from the ship were rowed along shallow coasts and up narrow creeks and rivers. The depth of the water was measured with a lead and line and marked on the new charts.

6 Artists drew detailed records of the people, animals, birds and plants of the Pacific Islands in the 18th century. Here an artist sketches a parrot.

7 Flowers and plants were collected and drawn on board the explorer's ships by natural history artists. Flowers were pressed to preserve them and seaweed hung up to dry. Careful accounts were made of all the new finds.

8 Plants were stored in small, portable greenhouses. Windows in the sides could be opened to let in the air. Small, rare trees were packed and carried in bamboo baskets.

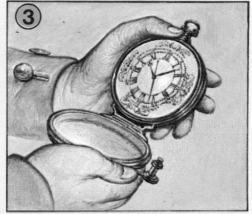

A Man-of-War

At the beginning of the 18th century, first-rate ships, like
this one, were the biggest and most powerful men-of-war
afloat. They were about 200 ft long and about 52 ft wide.
They had three gun decks with 104 guns and carried nearly
900 men, made up of officers, seamen, boys, servants and
marines.

The three gun decks were the main deck, where most of
the work was done; the middle deck, where the officers had
their wardroom and cabins; the seamen lived on the middle
and lower gun decks. The ceilings were low; a man had to
stoop to avoid banging his head. Above these decks were
the open quarter deck, the poop and the forecastle. Near
the waterline was the orlop deck and below it, in the lowest
part of the ship, was the hold, where the stores of food,
water and ammunition were kept.

The ship was driven by a vast number of sails spread on
a complicated network of masts, yards and rigging. The
three masts went down through the decks and rested on the
bottom of the ship. Capstans, turned by seamen pushing on
capstan bars, were used to haul on heavy ropes and the
anchor cables. The pumps kept the water in the bottom of
the ship down to a reasonable level.

1 The admiral and his officers
stood on the poop deck. From
here signals and orders were
given to the rest of the fleet.

2 Poop skylight.

3 The marines lined up here
during actions and fired on
enemy crews with muskets.

4 Mizzen mast.

5 The captain and officers
walked on the quarter deck.
The captain issued orders for
the running of the ship, heard
complaints and interviewed
anyone who had failed to carry
out his duties. Everybody on
board saluted when coming onto
the quarter deck.

6 Hammocks were lashed up and
put in netting round the ship's
upper decks when not in use.

7 The main mast, with its top
mast and top gallant sections, rose
about 175 ft above the deck.

8 The ship's boats rested on
chocks on the upper deck. They
were launched with tackles.

9 The sentry struck the bell
every half-hour. He also turned
three sand glasses, which
measured half-hour, two-hour and
four-hour periods.

10 The forecastle was the
station of the lieutenant of the
watch and the boatswain.

11 The foremast.

12 A short light gun called
a carronade.

13 The captain's quarters had
wide stern windows. Furniture
was quickly cleared and stowed
before a battle action.

14 The steering wheel, introduced
in ships about 1700, and the box
binnacle were on the quarter deck.

15 Officers' lavatories were
in the quarter galleries.

16 The admiral's spacious cabins were on the main deck. They were used by the captain when no admiral was on board.

17 Ladder between the decks.

18 Gun crews consisted of up to 15 men.

19 Men stationed in the waist had unskilled tasks. The blacksmith, carpenters, coopers, sailmakers and ropemakers also worked on this deck. The officers' hens, sheep, pigs and goats were kept here.

20 In the galley, with its boilers and ovens, the cook catered for the ship's company.

21 The ship had large anchors on both sides of the bows. When not in use, they were lashed firmly to the sides.

22 The wardroom where commissioned officers ate at the table and slept behind canvas screens between the guns.

23 The marines ate and slung their hammocks here.

24 The main capstan stood on the main and lower decks. As many as 260 men were needed to heave on the capstan bars to turn it when lifting big loads.

25 The fore capstan.

26 Petty officers and some landsmen lived on this deck. Tables and stools were ranged between the guns and hammocks slung from the beams.

27 The surgeon and his assistants cared for the sick and wounded in the sickbay.

28 Fresh air came through the bow gun ports into the sickbay.

29 Midshipmen and others were schooled and lived in the gun room on the lower deck.

30 The tiller, joined to the rudder, swept across the gun room when the wheel was turned.

31 The pumps were worked from this deck. They reached down into the well of the ship and drew water out of the bilges.

32 The heaviest guns, the 32-pounders, were on the lowest deck.

33 Anchor cables were secured to the bitts—upright timbers with a cross piece—to make them fast.

34 The anchor ropes passed through hawse holes in the bows. The ropes, called hawsers, then went across a manger. This prevented water from the hawsers washing over the lower deck.

35 The orlop deck was near the waterline. It was dark and airless.

36 Ship's biscuits were kept in the tin-lined breadroom.

37 The surgeon's cabin where he kept his medicines and surgical instruments.

38 Cabins for the gunners, boatswains and carpenters, and storerooms.

39 Mates, older midshipmen and assistant surgeons slept in the after cockpit. The surgeon treated the wounded here during a battle as it was below the range of gunfire.

40 The fore powder magazine supplied guns on the lower and middle decks. Powder was brought from the after magazine for the guns on the main and quarter decks and on the forecastle.

41 The rudder was hinged to the ship's stern. It was moved by turning the wheel to steer the ship and change course.

42 Casks of salted meat and fresh water and many other stores were kept in the hold. It was the home of many fat rats.

43 The anchor cables were stowed in the anchor tiers when not in use.

Fighting Men

A country's navy was owned and paid for by its king or ruler in ancient times. Armed ships were sent out to protect coastlines from invaders and defend merchant ships against pirates. They also attacked enemy coastal towns and transported troops during wars. Later most navies came under the control of their states, which ordered the ships to be built, appointed the officers and paid the seamen. At the time of the new colonies and the expanding empires of the western European nations, the navies were used to gain and hold new territory and to set up trading posts for their countries' merchant ships.

The marines were sea soldiers. They were trained to fight in naval battles and also help sail the ships. They had their own uniforms, similar to the armies of the times, and their own officers. They lived in separate quarters from the seamen on board ship, had their own weapons and ammunition stores. Unlike the seamen, they were not paid off at the end of a voyage but lived in barracks on shore.

Naval uniforms were first introduced for the officers of the French navy in 1665. The British navy adopted a uniform for its officers in 1748, while the seamen continued to wear ordinary clothes adapted for work at sea. They had bell-bottomed trousers which could be rolled up when washing decks, jackets and hats which were tarred to make them waterproof, rough shirts and neckerchiefs. Seamen were usually barefooted when working on board and wore their shoes only when going ashore. A seaman's uniform of blue cloth jacket, white trousers and a black and white hat was introduced in 1857. American naval uniforms were very similar to the British uniforms during the 1860s but were later changed to distinguish them. All navies gradually added epaulettes, gold braid and decorations to mark the different ranks of officers.

▲ The uniforms and dress worn by the officers, seamen and marines of a British naval ship in about 1805. The officers first wore uniforms in 1748. The crew wore ordinary clothes or "slops". Uniforms were first introduced for seamen in 1857.

The admiral had command of the whole fleet. He gave it orders while on a cruise and led it when going into battle. His flag was flown from one of the masts of his ship.

The captain was in charge of his ship and its crew. He was responsible for its navigation, equipment, stores and conduct in exercises and battle.

The lieutenant was next in rank to the captain and took command in his absence. He was in charge of a watch at sea and saw that the crew was at its battle stations.

The surgeon was responsible for detecting diseases on a ship and for treating the sick and wounded.

The purser was in charge of the food and drink provisions.

The midshipman carried out the orders of his superior officers and helped to run the ship.

Flags

Flags are flown from the masts of ships to show that it belongs to a country, navy or it is on certain business. The flag of an important person, such as a king or very senior officer is also hoisted to show that he is on board.

Ancient ships carried a symbol embroidered on their sails. Later the symbols were put on cloth flags and became part of a ship's decoration. Flags are also used for signalling. A national flag is lowered a third of the way down the mast and then raised again as a salute to a ship of another country.

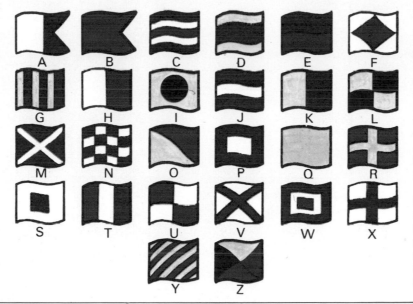

This international code of signals is used by most navies and all merchant shipping. Flags were used to pass messages between ships before the invention of radio. The Venetian navy had a flag code in the 15th century and the French and Spanish had signalling systems in the 16th century.

Groups of flags of the international code are used to spell out words and numbers. Many single flags also have a standard message. P, the Blue Peter, means a ship is about to sail.

he cook, often a wounded **eaman,** was in charge of the alley.
he sailmaker mended the sails.
he carpenter looked after the ship, repairing leaks and damage.
A member of a guncrew, stripped or action stations.

A seaman dressed for bad weather or for work in the boats.
A seamen dressed in his best clothes. Although seamen had no uniform, short blue jackets and neckerchiefs were often worn.
A member of a boarding party armed and ready for action.

A marine sergeant was in command of the marines in the absence of a senior officer.
A marine officer was in charge of marines on board a ship. He was responsible for their conduct, uniforms and weapons, and led them into battle.

A marine drummer summoned the marines to their stations during naval exercises and when going into battle.
A marine armed with a musket. As well as fighting in battles, marines acted as seamen and guarded ships when in port.

Manning the Ships

Life on board the sailing ships was hard, sometimes dangerous and usually badly paid. It was not always easy for ship owners and the navies to get men to serve on their ships. France had a system to man her navy whereby men had to spend a certain time in it. America, after the Revolution of 1776, had many volunteers as the pay was good. Britain and Russia recruited men into their navies by force. Merchant seamen were rounded up on shore and "pressed" into service. Criminals were taken from the gaols and even men too old to be of any use were taken aboard, as ships had to be fully manned in wartime. A ship's company was made up of men of all occupations and many nationalities. But it also had a core of experienced seamen who were relied on to sail the ship and enforce discipline.

Many men did volunteer for the navies, lured by the prospect of prize money from captured ships and some pay in advance. Usually seamen were paid only at the end of a voyage, which could last for several years. This was to prevent them from deserting when in foreign ports, but many still left their ships. Between 1774 and 1780, over 40,000 men deserted the British navy, twice the number who were killed in battle or died from disease. For naval officers, a life at sea was an honourable career, sometimes with rich rewards. Their quarters were often comfortable, their food better than the seamen's, and there were chances of promotion.

▲ **The captain and officers** went aboard a ship through the entry port. This was a door cut in the side of a warship on a level with the middle deck. The boatswain blew his whistle to "pipe them aboard" and to call the crew to attention. The seamen used ropes to help them climb up the ship's side on to the deck.

The press gang on Tower Hill in London. It was a familiar sight at the beginning of the 19th century when seafaring men were cudgelled into service in the British navy. In time of war, the press gang was necessary to get enough men for the ships.

A Sailor's Day

The seaman's day was divided into periods called watches. The length of a watch varied from country to country. On British ships, it lasted for four hours. The ship's bell was rung at the beginning of every watch and at half-hour intervals. A watch ended at "eight bells" when the four-hour sand glass was turned and counting began again.

The ship's company was divided into two or three groups, also called watches. The one on duty was called the "watch on deck" and was responsible for sailing and steering the ship. The group off duty was the "watch below". On a well-run naval ship, the day began at 3.30 am when the boatswain roused the sleeping "watch below". The decks were scrubbed, the sails set, hammocks stowed, weapons cleaned, brass polished and paint washed. Work went on throughout the day, with breaks for meals, until 8 pm.

▶ **The boatswain blew his whistle** to rouse the watch at the start of the day. By raising his fingers over the single hole in the round end of the whistle, he could produce a wide range of notes. An expert could make up to eight different notes, as well as varying the tone and length of sound. The boatswain blew certain signals to call the crew to certain duties and for manning the yards. He was responsible for the ship's rigging and sails and for seeing that the crew carried out their orders.

▲ **Every morning the ship's sails** were re-hoisted and others unfurled. In the evenings, some sails were taken down or furled so the ship sailed slowly and safely during the night. Some men went up the masts and out on to the spars to unfurl the sails. Others hoisted sails with ropes from the deck.

▲ **"Up spirits"** was the welcome order at about 11.00 am on British naval ships. In the 18th century, the British navy introduced a daily ration of half-a-pint of rum mixed with water. It was called grog. This replaced the ration of beer, which was often stale. Wine was also drunk when it was available.

▶ **Supper was served** at 5 pm to the watch below sitting on benches either side of a hanging table. The cook carried the food, cooked in a big pot, from the galley. Each group, or mess, on a large warship was under the command of a mess captain and had its own cook. Then there was time for yarns and jokes.

▶ **"Down hammocks"** was the order at about 8 pm on a naval ship. Hammocks were usually slung only 14 in apart. Each one was numbered and had an allotted place. A seaman had two hammocks: one clean and one in daily use.

▶ **Boatswain's mates took turns as lookouts** on the forecastle during the night watches. Lookouts were also positioned in the rigging and on the quarter and poop decks.
   During the night, the lights were put out. In good weather, the ship was quiet. The only sounds were the creaking of the rigging, the tapping of ropes, and the cry of "all's well" from the lookouts at half-hourly intervals. When the watch was changed, those sleeping below were called up for duty on deck.

Crime and Punishment

Discipline on board naval ships had to be strict. The kind and number of punishments for offences varied from ship to ship and depended very much on the captain or officers.

The most common offences by the crew were getting drunk, fighting and refusing to obey orders. Men guilty of minor crimes were put in the bilboes, given extra duties or flogged. For serious crimes, such as mutiny, desertion or cowardice in the face of the enemy, the offenders were tried and sentenced by a court martial. If found guilty, they were punished by a flogging through the fleet or death by hanging on board their own ships.

Twelve Lashes

Flogging was a frequent punishment for minor offences. Ships' logs show how often it occurred and record the offence and the number of lashes. "Twelve lashes for insolence", reads one entry. The official instruction issued by the British naval authorities in 1781 limited the number of lashes to 12 but captains often ordered far more. The floggings were carried out by the boatswain's mates or members of the crew.

There were different punishments for officers. Junior officers, including midshipmen who were sometimes only ten years old, were "mastheaded" for minor offences. This meant they were sent up the mast and had to stay there, without food. Other punishments included the stoppage of shore leave when in port. Senior officers were put under arrest to await a court martial, which might result in dismissal from the navy.

Instruments of Punishment

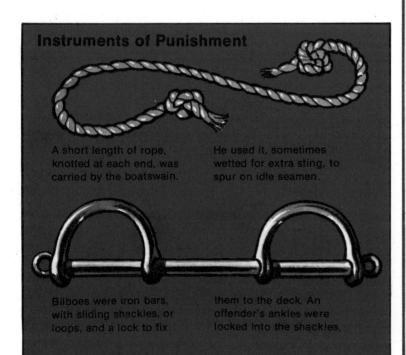

A short length of rope, knotted at each end, was carried by the boatswain.

He used it, sometimes wetted for extra sting, to spur on idle seamen.

Bilboes were iron bars, with sliding shackles, or loops, and a lock to fix them to the deck. An offender's ankles were locked into the shackles.

Discipline in the Navy

◀ **A man was hanged** on board a ship only after he had been tried and sentenced to death by a court martial. The sailor was taken back aboard his ship with a rope round his neck. This was knotted to a rope on a yard arm. A party of sailors manned the rope. When a gun fired the signal of death, they ran forward and hoisted the unfortunate man into the air to hang until dead.

▲ **Flogging through the fleet** was one of the worst punishments. The culprit was tied up and rowed in a boat to each ship in the fleet. He was flogged by a man from each ship and often maimed for life.

▲ **Running the gauntlet** was an unofficial punishment, awarded for theft or a crime against the crew. The guilty man was stripped to the waist and forced to walk past the members of the crew who beat him with knotted cords.

▶ **Sailors were put in the bilboes,** which were like stocks, for minor offences such as getting drunk. The men had to sit on deck with their legs clamped in the iron shackles so they could not move. To add to their discomfort, they were laughed at by their fellow sailors whenever they passed the bilboes.

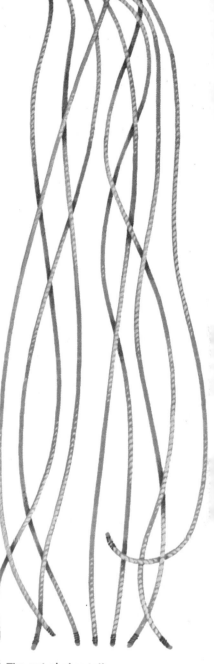

Floggings happened so often that they were part of life on board some ships. They were held at 11 a.m. on the quarter deck and the whole ship's company turned out and were obliged to watch. It was hoped that the flogging would act as a warning against bad behaviour.

Although no seaman was supposed to receive more than 12 lashes, a severe crime was often punished with many more. If the offender shouted or swore, he was gagged.

1 The prisoner is stripped to the waist and his hands are tied above his head to the grating.

2 The boatswain's mate uses a cat o' nine tails to carry out the flogging.

3 The ship's surgeon stands by to feel the man's pulse.

4 The captain holds the paper setting out the offence and the punishment.

5 Two young midshipmen, wearing round hats, stand in line with the other officers on the quarter deck to watch the ceremony.

6 Seamen crowd round for a good view of the punishment.

7 Marines are lined up on the poop deck. A non-commissioned officer is on the right, with a drummer next to him.

▲ **The cat o' nine tails** was a whip used for flogging. It was made on board ship, copying the official pattern.

It consisted of a length of broom handle, about 2 ft long, covered with red baize. Nine pieces of log line, or thin rope, about 3 ft long were attached to the handle. The tails sometimes had knots tied in them to make the flogging more painful. Twelve lashes from a cat was enough to cut the skin of a man's back.

Life and Death on Board

Sailing ships were crowded, often dirty and always damp. The seamen were huddled together in dark, airless conditions between the decks. They lived on bad food, stale drinking water and large quantities of sour beer, wine and rum. Many died of diseases which were caught in foreign ports or were caused by the bad conditions and quickly spread through the ships.

Seamen had all sorts of accidents. They were bruised and battered by ropes, blocks and flapping sails. They strained themselves heaving on ropes and pushing on the capstan bars. They fell from the rigging and spars on to the decks when handling the sails. Worse still, they fell or were washed overboard and often drowned before they could be rescued.

Battle wounds

During a battle the guncrews were sometimes badly burned by an accidental explosion of gunpowder. They were also wounded or killed by enemy cannon balls and wood splinters. A shot fired at close range made a clean hole in a ship but one fired from a distance caused more casualties from the shattered timber.

A surgeon on board a ship cared for his patients as best he could. But he was often badly trained and had little real medical knowledge. Cutting off a wounded arm or leg was often thought to be better than trying to heal it. There were no anaesthetics or pain-killing medicines. Only the strongest survived the rough treatment.

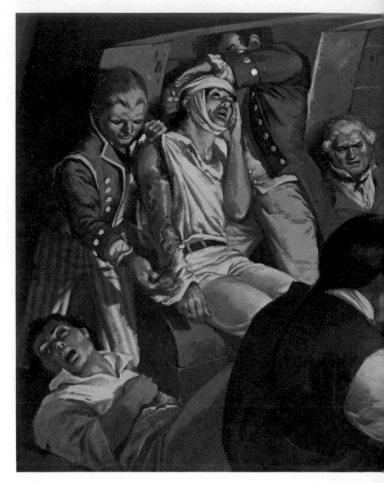

▲ **During a battle** the wounded were treated on the dimly-lit lowest deck. This was below the waterline and out of the line of gunfire. A sail was spread over the treatment area and sea chests were used for operating tables. The surgeon and his assistants worked as fast as they could, while the injured waited their

The Surgeon's Tools

A surgeon appointed to a new ship brought with him his own box of instruments. Among them was a tourniquet. This was put on a shattered limb and screwed tight to stop the flow of blood. There were also knives, saws, splints for broken bones, syringes and bandages to treat everyday accidents as well as serious burns and bullet wounds.

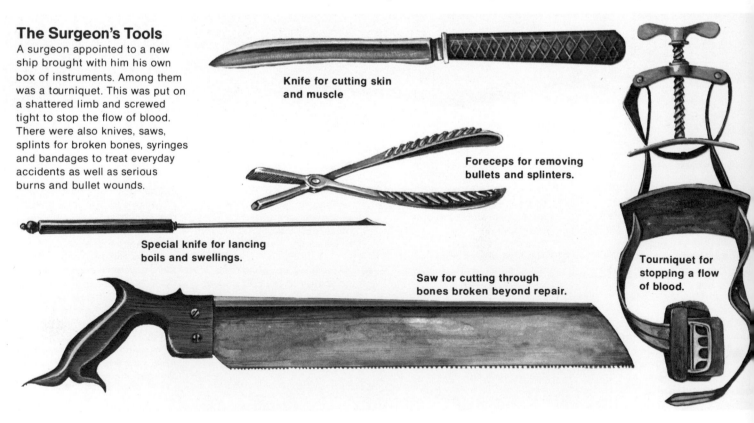

Knife for cutting skin and muscle

Foreceps for removing bullets and splinters.

Special knife for lancing boils and swellings.

Saw for cutting through bones broken beyond repair.

Tourniquet for stopping a flow of blood.

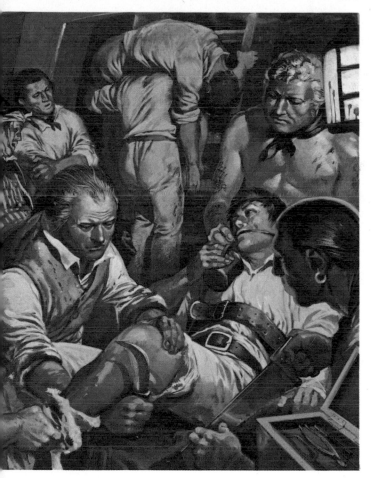

The Ship's "Heads"

The "heads" were the seamen's lavatories, so called because they were at the front, or head, of the ship. On the open deck, they were exposed to the wind and sometimes washed by the waves in a rough sea. There were probably fewer than ten heads on a large ship. The officers had their own arrangements. There were no baths or showers and all washing was done in seawater.

rn and more were carried down. ey cut off shattered limbs, andaged wounds and treated urns while the ship rolled with e waves and the guns fired on the decks over their heads. When a man had a limb removed, he was given rum or brandy to deaden the pain. He chewed on leather to stop him screaming.

A Sailor's Funeral

The officer-of-the-watch was told as soon as a sailor died on board a ship. He immediately informed the captain.

The dead sailor's messmates prepared him for burial. His own hammock was taken down and his body wrapped in it.

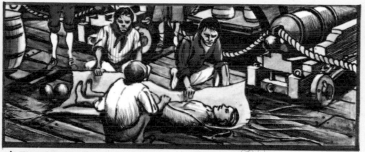

▲ **The dead sailor** is laid out on deck in his hammock. His messmates help the sailmaker as he stitches it up.

Two cannon balls are used to weight down the body. It is then placed on a grating and covered with the national flag.

▲ **Next morning,** the ship's bell is tolled and the crew gather to watch. The captain reads the funeral service.

One sailor takes off the flag as others slide the body and grating into the sea. The grating is hauled back on board.

There were medicine chests n all ships. They contained mple pills and powders for l the diseases and illnesses kely to be suffered by seamen. olid medicines were crushed ith a pestle in a small marble mortar. Powdered medicines were weighed on scales. If there was no surgeon on board a ship, the captain gave out the medicines, following the instructions in the medical handbook which went with the chest.

▲ **After the funeral,** the dead man's clothing, books and possessions are auctioned amongst the ship's company.

When the ship returns to its home port, the money made from the sale is handed over to his widow or family.

Weapons

The success of a battle at sea usually depended on the skill of the admirals and the number of guns carried by each fleet. The guncrew of a 32 pounder, the heaviest cannon in general use afloat, was made up of 15 men. They were responsible for two guns, one on each side of the ship. The guncrew had a first and second captain. When firing guns on both sides of the ship, each captain was in charge of one gun and the crew split their duties between them. Guncrews were numbered and had other jobs to do. Some formed parties for boarding enemy ships, others worked the pumps if enemy shot caused a leak in the ship; and others put out fires on deck. They trimmed the sails, fetched powder from the powder store, fetched lanterns from the galleys and opened the gun ports.

Preparing for Action

Before the guns could be fired, the decks had to be cleared of furniture. In a good ship, this took only 15 minutes. The cook put out the galley fire and lit special lanterns for the dark, smoky decks. Men threw down water and sand, and filled the fire buckets. Fire on board a ship was always a danger during a battle.

When all the guns on one side of the ship fired at the same time, it was called a broadside. Well-trained crews could fire three broadsides in one-and-a-half minutes. But after several shots, the guns got hot and jumped about so this rate of firing could not be kept up for long.

Grape shot, a bundle of musket balls

Chain shot, two shots joined by chain

Cannon ball

Bar shot, two half balls joined with a bar

◄ **The carronade,** a gun developed at Carron in Scotland in the 18th century, was short, light and destructive at short range.

► **A guncrew prepares to fire.** They pull on the ropes and heave at hand spikes to move the loaded cannon into place, with its muzzle pointing out through the gun port. The gun captain aims the cannon at the target. When the order is given to fire, he pulls the flintlock trigger. The spark lights the gunpowder in the touchhole. This lights the powder cartridge which forces out the shot. The gun jumps back but is held by ropes.

◄ **Many deadly shapes of shot** were fired from cannon. Most common was the round, cast iron ball. Bar shot and chain shot was aimed at an enemy ship's masts and rigging. If this was cut, the ship could not sail away and escape.

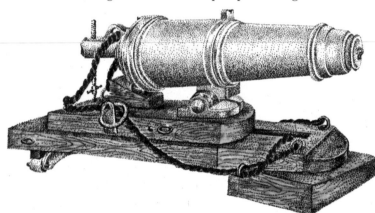

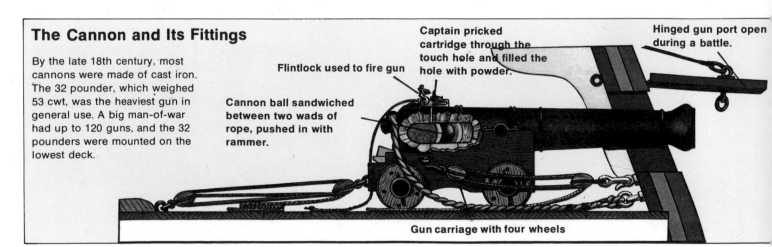

The Cannon and Its Fittings

By the late 18th century, most cannons were made of cast iron. The 32 pounder, which weighed 53 cwt, was the heaviest gun in general use. A big man-of-war had up to 120 guns, and the 32 pounders were mounted on the lowest deck.

Flintlock used to fire gun

Captain pricked cartridge through the touch hole and filled the hole with powder.

Hinged gun port open during a battle.

Cannon ball sandwiched between two wads of rope, pushed in with rammer.

Gun carriage with four wheels

Small Arms

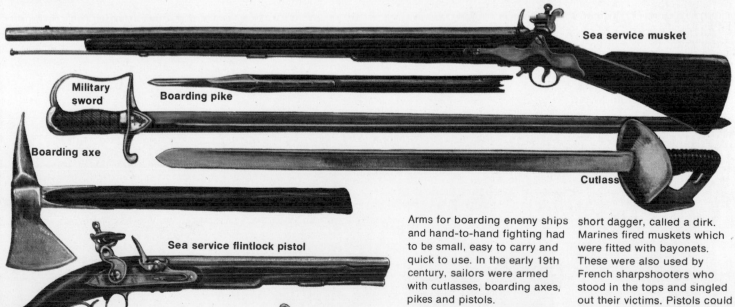

Sea service musket

Military sword

Boarding pike

Boarding axe

Cutlass

Sea service flintlock pistol

Dirk

Arms for boarding enemy ships and hand-to-hand fighting had to be small, easy to carry and quick to use. In the early 19th century, sailors were armed with cutlasses, boarding axes, pikes and pistols.

Pikes were at least 8 ft long and difficult to use at close quarters. Some men carried a short dagger, called a dirk. Marines fired muskets which were fitted with bayonets. These were also used by French sharpshooters who stood in the tops and singled out their victims. Pistols could not be re-loaded quickly so sailors carried several in their belts.

Battle Tactics

A ship preparing for battle was a scene of frantic but disciplined activity. The decks were cleared, the gun ports opened, the guns loaded and run out. The wind was vitally important in battle tactics. A sailing ship had to use its sails to manoeuvre into a good attacking position. If it could cross an enemy's bows or stern, it could fire all the guns along its sides, while the enemy had only a few guns pointing directly ahead or astern. The amount of sails set was also important. If a ship heeled, or leaned, far over with the wind, its guns on the windward side pointed up and shot might go over the enemy's masts at long range. The guns on the other side pointed down, or the lower gunports had to be closed to stop the sea coming in.

Most sea battles were fought at close range, with guns pounding away at the wooden hulls and rigging. Manuals of battle tactics recommended that a fleet should sail into the attack in a straight, close line. This method was adopted by fleet commanders of most countries.

▲ This shows how the sails of a square-rigged ship were turned to catch the wind. The wind is the blue arrow. When the wind was blowing from behind, the sails filled and the ship was pushed forward. If the wind was blowing from one side, the sails were turned and the ship was still pushed forward, but slightly sideways as well. A ship could not sail straight into the wind; it would be blown backwards. If a captain wanted to go in the direction the wind was blowing from, he sailed a zig-zag course.

Single Ship Action

These pictures are of a battle between the American frigate *Constitution* and the British frigate *Java* in 1812. The direction of the wind is shown by the blue arrows.

The *Constitution* had been successful in several previous actions. The *Java*, recently captured from the French and renamed, had a raw crew with no experience of firing its guns.

As the sails and rigging of the British *Java* were soon shot away, it became almost helpless and could not take evasive action or escape. The *Constitution* although damaged, could sail round to manoeuvre into good positions and make the best use of its guns. At the end of the battle, the Americans boarded the *Java* and took prisoners. The *Java* was set on fire and later exploded.

③ ▲ The Americans turn and come up for another broadside. The *Java* drifts on but, still firing, damages the enemy's rigging.

① ▲ The *Constitution* overtakes the *Java* on its windward side. A broadside from the Americans shoots away the *Java*'s fore mast.

④ ▲ The *Constitution* sails out of range to repair its rigging. The *Java*, all masts gone, tries to hoist sails on the broken stumps.

② ▲ The *Constitution* rounds the *Java*'s bows, raking it with shot. The *Java*'s starboard guns are smothered by the fallen mast.

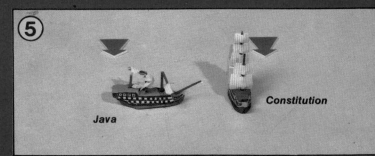

⑤ ▲ The *Constitution* sails down wind to cross the *Java*'s bows for the last attack. The British haul down the flag and surrender.

The Battle of the Nile

These pictures show the French and British ships during the Battle of the Nile in 1798. The blue arrows indicate the direction of the wind.

The French fleet anchored in a bay off the mouth of the River Nile in Egypt. Its admiral, de Breuys, probably thought it was safe and in a good position to repel any attack.

The British squadron, commanded by Nelson, found them there on August 1. Nelson ordered his ships to prepare for battle. At dusk, the squadron sailed in line into the bay towards the head of the French line of ships.

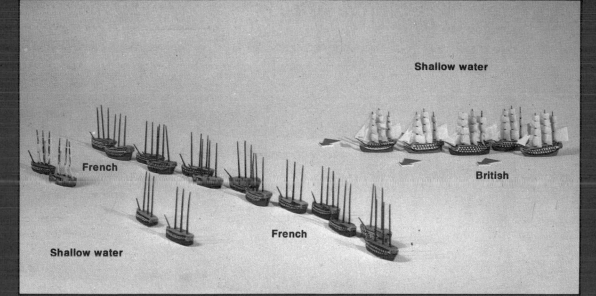

The leading British ship attacked the head of the French line, firing its cannons at close range. Followed by other ships of the squadron, it rounded the French line and sailed down the other side. This pincer manoeuvre surprised the French admiral. He did not expect any enemy ships to sail between his fleet and the land where the water was shallow. Only his guns on the seaward side were prepared for action and ready to fire.

Other ships of the British squadron sailed towards the centre of the French line to attack there. The battle continued into the night, the darkness lit by gunfire and burning ships. Some French ships cut their anchor cables and tried to escape.

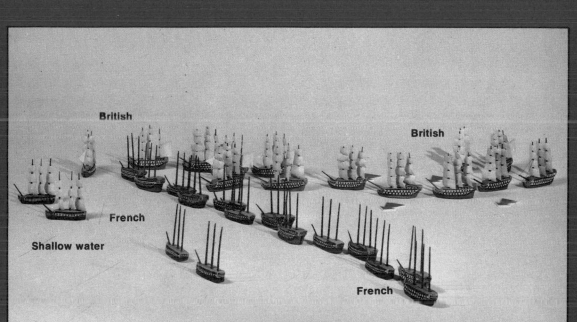

The British squadron broke through the line of the French fleet, attacking on both sides. The French flagship was set alight and later blew up, killing the admiral and most of the crew. Nelson was wounded but watched the battle after his head had been bandaged.

The French fought bravely, pounding the British ships with their guns. One by one they hoisted sails and tried to escape or lowered their flags and surrendered. The last of the British line had gone aground at the entrance to the bay and its captain was forced to watch the action from afar.

By morning, the battle was over. All but four of the French ships had been captured or sunk.

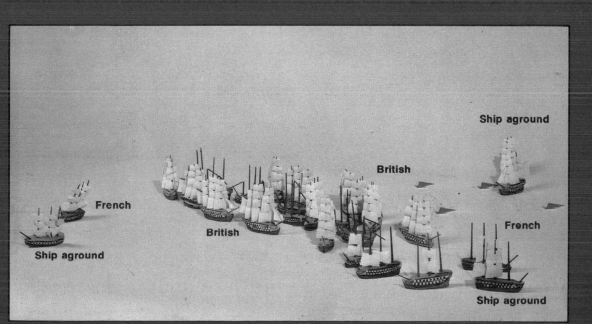

Shipwreck and Rescue

Well-built sailing ships were seldom wrecked in open seas. They could weather most gales and were designed to sail through the biggest waves. It was when they came near the land that they faced danger. Out-of-date charts, careless navigation and the lack of warnings marking underwater rocks and sand banks caused many ships to be wrecked and many people drowned. A sailing ship depended on the wind. If there was none, a ship was becalmed and even with all its sails set, it drifted helplessly with the current unless anchored.

Fire was always a danger on board a wooden ship. A spark from the galley or a dropped lantern could easily start a blaze. Fanned by the wind, it soon spread throughout the ship.

A well-built ship could survive almost any weather but a hurricane could cause great damage. Masts and spars were carried away by the winds and sails split.

Badly-drawn and incorrect charts often led ships to run on to unmarked rocks and sand banks. The first known charts date from 1300 but were not drawn to scale and distances were inaccurate.

Icebergs drifting with the ocean currents caused many shipwrecks. Only a small part of their bulk is above the water and they are often hidden by fog.

How People Were Saved

If a ship was wrecked or broke up in heavy seas, there were various ways the crew and passengers could be saved. Here are some of them.

▼ **Survivors of a ship** wrecked at sea sometimes made rafts on which to escape. If there was time, they lashed together spars and barrels. Ships seldom had enough boats for all the crew and passengers and they were difficult to launch in a storm.

This 18th-century English lifeboat had a crew of twelve There was a steering oar at each end so it could be rowed either way. A thick band of cork round the lifeboat kept it afloat.

An Englishman, George Manby, invented this lifesaving device. A cannon ball, with a line attached, was fired over the wreck.

Men on the wreck pulled a thick rope aboard. People, in a sling hanging from the rope, were pulled ashore, one at a time.

he Eddystone Lighthouse was ne of the first in England to ark dangerous rocks. It was built n rocks off the coast but was wept away by a gale in 1702.

Strong tides and currents along coasts swept many ships on to rocks. If there was no wind, a ship drifted helplessly into the shallow water and was stranded when the tide went out.

Careless navigation caused many shipwrecks. One 18th-century captain, sailing in the East Indies, was 1,000 miles out in his calculations of his position.

ship might be blown on to the shore if it dragged e anchor. This meant the anchor failed to hook rmly in a sandy or muddy seabed and was dragged y the ship.

Bad discipline occasionally caused a ship to be wrecked. Discontented sailors broke open casks of rum and brandy. Soon drunk, they refused to obey orders.

Old, patched-up leaking merchant ships went down in storms. Shipowners tried to save money on repairs to the hulls and rigging and loaded ships with too much cargo.

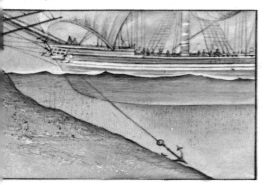

Salvaged from Wrecks

The captain, passengers and crew of a ship took many personal belongings with them. In the past, people living on rocky coasts prayed that ships would be wrecked because of the treasures that were washed up on the shore. Today men salvaging wrecks in a more scientific way can learn much about the way ships were built and life on board them.

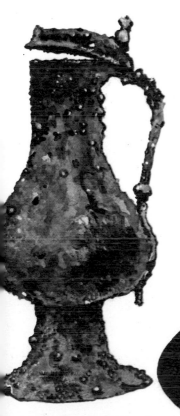

A pewter chamberpot found in the wreck of the British ship, the *Association*. The ship sank off the Isles of Scilly in 1707.

is pewter jug was recovered m the English warship, *Mary ose*, after remaining for 500 ars underwater.

A felt hat found in a sailor's chest. It was among the huge number of articles saved from the 17th-century Swedish warship, the *Wasa*.

Pirates and Buccaneers

Piracy began in the earliest days of seafaring. Men could make a good living plundering any trading ships they met at sea, whether friends or enemies. It was almost a recognized profession. Piracy flourished in the Middle Ages and again after the Crusades when new trade was building up in the Mediterranean and with the East.

The Barbary corsairs operated from the north African states which came under the rule of the Great Turk of Constantinople. They attacked Christian ships, taking prisoners to row their galleys. Some of the most successful corsair leaders were Christians and often accepted encouragement from one Christian country to attack another. They plundered merchant shipping until 1830 when the area was colonized by the French.

Buccaneers

Men from England, France, Holland and Germany banded together in the 16th century to form the Brotherhood of the Coast. Their ships were based in the West Indies and they waged ruthless and unofficial war on the Spanish settlements and ships. One famous commander was Henry Morgan who plundered Panama. Later he was knighted and became the governor of Jamaica. The buccaneers dispersed about the end of the 17th century. Some of them probably turned honest. Others began to prey on the shipping in the Indian Ocean and the Red Sea.

Privateers were privately-owned warships which attacked enemy shipping. They were equipped by merchants and licensed by their country to make prizes of enemy ships. The captains and crews made a good living from selling the ships and cargoes when they reached home. Privateering was abolished by the sovereigns of the European countries who signed a treaty in 1856.

▶ **A pirate is hanged.** Captain William Kidd, who was born in Scotland, became a privateer and settled in New York. He turned pirate and seized a ship in the Indian Ocean belonging to the Great Mogul, the emperor of Delhi. When he returned to America, he was arrested and taken to London. There he was executed, in 1701, and his body dipped in tar. It was hung up as a warning to others.

▶ **One 18th-century pirate flag** was decorated with a death's head, a battle-axe and an hour-glass on a black background. The hour-glass was supposed to show how much time captured seamen were allowed to make their decision—either they joined the pirates in their roving life or they refused and were put to death.

◀ **Blackbeard the Pirate** was born in England. His real name was Edward Teach. Daring and ruthless, he became the terror of the east coast of America. When going into battle, he put two slow-burning matches in twists of his beard. This was to increase his already frightening appearance and unnerve his enemies. He was killed in 1718 after a desperate fight with the captain of a British man-of-war.

▶ **Pirates boarding a merchant ship** to plunder it for goods on board. They chased a likely ship and often tried to trick the crew by flying the flag of a friendly country. Then they fired shots to prevent the merchant ship from escaping.

The pirates seized the ship and demanded a list of cargo on board. Then they questioned crew and passengers. Anyone who refused to give away information was often brutally treated.

In the 17th and 18th centuries ships and crews were often ransomed. In the 19th century pirates were more afraid of being caught and executed so they tried to cover their tracks by killing their prisoners and destroying the ships.

There were a few women pirates. The two most famous, Mary Read and Ann Bonney, sailed in pirate ships along the Atlantic coast of America. They fought just as fiercely as the men. Eventually they were captured and put in prison in Jamaica. Mary died there but Ann escaped and disappeared.

▲ **Benito de Soto**, a Portuguese pirate, called his ship *Black Joke*. He plundered and sank many ships before retiring to Gibraltar. There he was arrested and was condemned to death.

Wreckers

Islanders collecting cargo from a ship wrecked on a rocky coast. In England an old law allowed cargo to be salvaged from a wreck if no living thing remained on board. The story goes that survivors were killed so the wreck could be plundered. Poor people living on the coasts certainly welcomed the wealth that the shipwrecks brought them.

Whaling

"Beware the sperm's jaw and the right whale's flukes", was an old saying amongst whaling men. There are many different types of whales but the sperm and right whales were the ones most frequently hunted in the early days of whaling. Hunting them was hard and dangerous work but a successful expedition made large profits.

Sperm whales, as much as 60 ft long, have huge jaws and can bite a small whaling boat in half. As they can only see ahead and to each side, whaling boats approached them from behind. Right whales have no teeth but their powerful tails, with fins called flukes, could overturn or smash a boat.

Whales are mammals and have to come to the surface of the sea to breathe, or "blow". They spout a puff of warm air as much as 20 ft high. In cold weather this looks like a column of smoke or water. Whaling men watched for this spout from the mastheads of their ships. At the cry of "there she blows", small boats were launched from the ships and the chase began. The whales were hunted for their oil, blubber and for ambergris—a grey, greasy material from their stomachs—used for making perfume.

When a whale was sighted, small rowing boats raced to attack it. The harpooner stabbed it with a lance attached to a long rope. A boat might be towed for miles before it could come up to the whale and kill it.

Then the ship sailed up to the dead whale. It was tied to the side of the ship so it could be cut up and the valuable parts hoisted on to the deck.

1 Sailors cut a sperm whale's head in two before lifting it onto the deck. The lower part contains a clear, valuable oil which is collected in buckets. This oil was used to make soap and candles.

2 A sperm whale's teeth are as much as 1 ft long. The jaw is cut from the whale and the teeth removed from the gums by sailors on deck.

3 The thick layer of fat, called blubber, is cut off the dead whale with special long knives while it lies alongside the ship. The blubber strips are lifted on board and boiled in huge kettles set in brick ovens, called try works, to extract the oil. This is then ladled into casks to cool. The blubber from a large whale produced as many as 100 barrels of oil.

Line Fishing

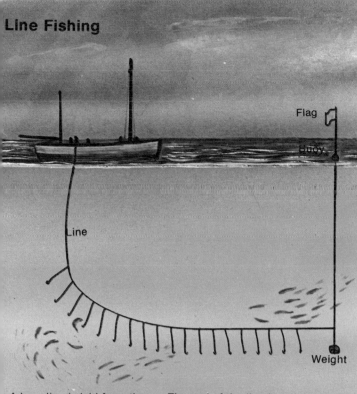

A long line is laid from the ship across the tide so that the short lines, with baited hooks, drift clear.

The end of the line is weighted to keep it underwater. A float, or buoy, with a small flag, marks the end of the drifting fishing line.

Fishing

Fishing has been one of the main ways of getting food from the very earliest times. There are three principal methods of catching fish, all still in use today.

The line is perhaps the oldest method. It consists of a long line with short lines, called snoods, tied to it at intervals. On the ends of the short lines are hooks with bait, such as shellfish, to attract the fish. Line fishing is always done during the day.

The drift net is cast from a ship wherever there are signs of fish. The net forms a wall, about two miles long and drifts with the tide. Drift nets are laid between sunset and dawn because the fish caught in them seem to be affected by the changing light.

Trawling is the most important method of fishing today. The net is dragged along the bottom of the sea to catch fish which swim close to the seabed.

Fishing boats developed according to the type of fishing they were needed for and the kind of seas and winds they were sailed in. From about 1700, ketches of various sizes were common in European waters. The sturdy, graceful hull and two powerful masts were strong enough to withstand rough seas and the weight of the nets. Steam engines and the overfishing of the North Sea put the sailing trawlers out of business.

Drift Net Fishing

The drift net hangs in the water, about 12 ft below the surface, moving with the tide.

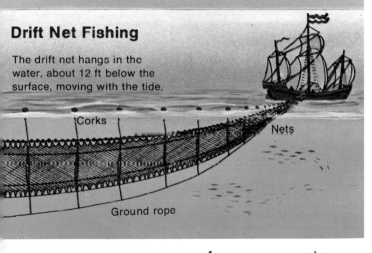

It is used to catch fish swimming near the surface, such as herring and mackerel.

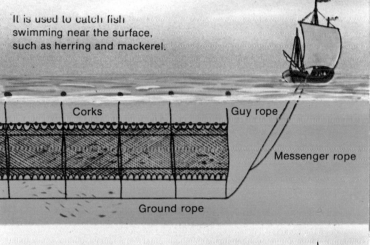

Trawl Fishing

A trawl is a long bag of netting, about 3 or 4 ft wide. The mouth of the trawl is kept open by a beam.

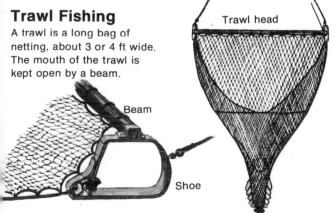

The trawl is dragged along the seabed by a fishing boat to catch such fish as cod, plaice and haddock. Once the fish are in the narrow part they cannot swim out.

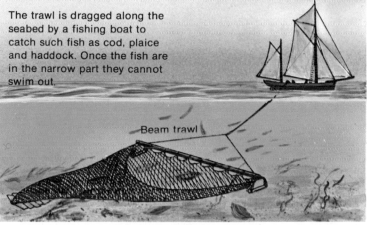

Clipper Ships

For over 200 years, British ships claimed the sole right to trade with British India and the Far East. Large, well-armed ships carried valuable cargoes of silks, spices, jewels and carpets. Safety was far more important than speed. A voyage from Britain to India took six months and one to China might last a year.

Early in the 19th century, fast American ships were crossing the Atlantic. They had long, slim hulls and were sailed as fast as possible, even in bad weather. When the British trade routes were opened to other countries, larger, faster ships, called clippers, were built in the United States. They reduced the voyage to China to seven months and, gradually, to four months. At that time, China was the only country growing large amounts of tea. It was thought that long sea voyages ruined the flavour, so the first ship to bring the new season's crop of tea to Europe earned a large bonus.

The Gold Rush

Then, in 1848, gold was found in California. Thousands of people rushed there in search of fortunes. American clippers, crowded with diggers, goods and equipment, raced to the new mining towns and camps. Two years later, gold was discovered in Australia and a second rush began.

When British owners found their ships were too slow to compete for trade, they ordered clippers to be built in British shipyards. Soon they proved they could match the speed of the American ships and challenged them to many races. France and Sweden joined in the tea trade.

By the middle of the century, the new steamships were proving faster and more reliable than sailing ships. These puffing "kettles" took over the North Atlantic passenger routes and American clippers dropped out of the trade. British ships continued to race each other home from China but when the Suez Canal was opened in 1869, steamships could make the much shorter journey in two months. The clippers soon lost the tea trade but some changed to the Australian wool route. These beautiful sailing ships were reduced to carrying cargoes for which there was no hurry. The days of the clippers were over.

▲ **Passengers on emigrant ships** lived in dark, crowded conditions. They had to cook their own food on deck. When the weather was bad, the hatches were closed and the people stayed below decks, eating cold food. Many emigrants died on the long voyages from Europe to Australia and New Zealand.

▲ **Gold-seekers on the deck** of a clipper racing to California. High fares could be charged for fast voyages to the new gold mining towns where thousands of people rushed to stake their claims. In 1849, the first year of the California gold rush, 800 ships sailed round Cape Horn and northwards across the Pacific to the east coast of the United States.

◀ **This huge German ship,** called the *Preussen*, was built in Hamburg in 1902. It had a steel hull, 433 ft long, and could carry 8,000 tons of cargo. It was the biggest and only five-masted fully-rigged ship in the world.

The *Preussen* had two steam engines on deck to raise the anchor and lift cargo in and out of the holds. It was part of the German merchant fleet which was built on the lines of British and American ships.

The clippers set up incredible speed records for ships of the time. Crowding on as many sails as the masts could carry, the captains raced each other home from China. They tried several different routes to make the best use of the trade winds and strong ocean currents. The speed of a voyage across thousands of miles of open sea depended on the captain. He urged his crew of between 20 and 40 seamen to work hard at changing or adjusting the sails to every change in the wind.

The hulls of clipper ships were long and slim with overhanging bows. They were very different from earlier cargo ships which had bluff bows and fat, rounded hulls designed to carry large cargoes. The clippers were built for speed and had tall masts which could carry a huge amount of sail. They were developed from fast, little ships built at Baltimore, in the United States, to outsail the slower, sturdy British warships.

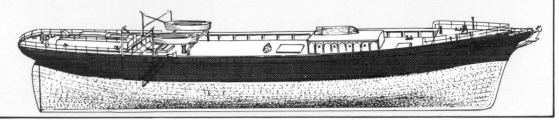

Time Chart

This chart shows some of the changes that the sailing ship has undergone since reed boats were built about 6,000 years ago. In northern Europe, ships developed slowly, often borrowing ideas from eastern Mediterranean ships. The masts and sails became more elaborate. The large oar (steering board) was replaced by a rudder. The steering oar gave the name of starboard to the ship's right when facing forward. The left side was called the larboard but was later changed to port. Many sailing ships in other parts of the world have retained their traditional designs of hulls and sails.

The Egyptians built one of the earliest known types of sailing ship. It was made of bundles of papyrus reeds bound tightly together with twine. It had a woven reed shelter near the stern and was steered with an oar. It was sailed on rivers but not in the open sea.

A ship common in northwest Europe from 200 A.D. It was double-ended, with one mast and a square sail which could be lowered when not in use. It had a steering oar on the right-hand side.

After 1200 A.D. the single-masted ship became bigger. It had raised decks, called castles, fore and aft to shelter the crew and provide fighting platforms. There were sometimes flagstaffs on the castles.

Later castles became permanent structures and the flagstaffs developed into the fore and mizzen masts. Sails were set on them and on the bowsprit which extended from the forecastle.

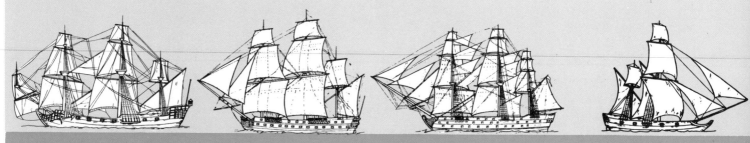

In the late 17th century big ships had three masts. The mizzen mast had a square topsail but the mizzen yard still carried a lateen sail.

In the early 18th century extra triangular sails, called stay sails, were set between the masts. Reefing replaced bonnets as the way of reducing sail.

Late 18th-century warships and merchant ships were heavily armed. The sail on the mizzen mast had booms at top and bottom.

An early type of ketch was a small ship with two masts, used for coastal trading. This ship is rigged without its foremast.

The tea clipper had tall masts and a great spread of sail. Its long, slender hull was built to sail very fast in all weathers with light, valuable cargoes, such as tea.

In the late 19th century the hull of the fully-rigged ship was built of steel not wood. Each mast carried several sails. They were not reefed but taken in with the help of winches.

The four-masted barques which sailed round Cape Horn carried wool, wheat and manure. These ships, which were also called "windjammers", were still carrying cargoes in the 1920s.

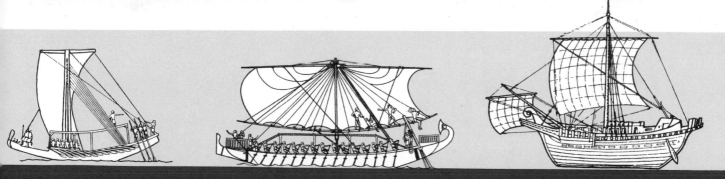

An Egyptian sailing boat of about 3000 B.C. It has three oars at the stern to steer the ship. The mast was two spars joined at the top, with one sail.

An Egyptian sea-going ship of about 1500 B.C. It had one steering oar. A thick rope joined bow and stern to prevent them drooping, as the ship had no keel. The mast was one spar and carried a wide square sail. There were raised decks front and back for lookout and helmsman.

A Roman merchant ship of about 50-200 A.D. It had a square sail and a triangular sail could be set above it, and a second sail set forward.

A large 16th-century ship. Its four masts carried top masts and extra sails. Gun ports were introduced into the sides and heavy guns could then be mounted on the lower deck.

Triangular lateen sails were common in Mediterranean ships. They were used on galleys which had many oars and three masts. These sails were later adopted for northern European ships.

In the 17th century there was little difference between big ships built in north and south Europe. They now had a spritsail topmast at the bows and a square mizzen sail.

The brigantine had two masts with square-rigged sails and two triangular foresails. This rig was a favourite with pirates and sea brigands.

The schooner had square top sails on its two upper masts and fore and aft sails beneath. It sailed well and was easy to handle.

The lugger was a small fast type of boat. It sailed close to the wind. It carried stores to bigger ships and was used by smugglers.

The cutter had a slender hull, one mast and a long bowsprit. It was fast and was used by smugglers and government forces chasing them.

The Arab dhow, still used today, has changed its shape little since the Middle Ages. It was usually sailed by day, and the mizzen sail was only hoisted on long runs in good weather.

The Indonesian proa had side galleries for the oars and square sails. It had rudders on both sides of the stern.

The traditional Chinese trading junk had a flat bottom and square sails made of reed matting.

Index

Numbers in **bold** refer to illustrations